YES I HAVE PERFECTIONISM DEAL. WITH. IT

Copyright © 2021 by Yes I Have Anxiety, Inc.

All rights reserved.

Thank you for purchasing an authorized edition of this book and for complying with copyright laws by not reproducing, scanning, or distributing any part of it in any form without permission.

Consumer Use Disclaimer: The "Yes I Have" book series was created in light-hearted, relatable fun to create distractions from things individuals may be dealing with. All "Yes I Have" books are not intended to diagnose medical conditions nor provide a cure for any medical conditions. This book is not meant to be a replacement for real medical intervention if needed.

ISBN: 978-1-7364840-9-8

First Edition: December 2021

Yes I Have Anxiety, Inc.
Grove, Ok 74345

This book is dedicated to our Jade-er-ade. She is a very loved family friend who helped us keep everything in order during some of the most challenging times in our lives. She was always able to keep everything running smoothly! We couldn't have made it without you! Thank you, Jade, for being such a great friend, mentor, and support system to our family. Thank you for sticking by our side even when we made all the messes and threw all the fits growing up. A special thank you for teaching us the difference between just clean and "JADE CLEAN"! We will forever be grateful for you.

With so much love,

The Stephen6Pack

Fill in The Keyboard.

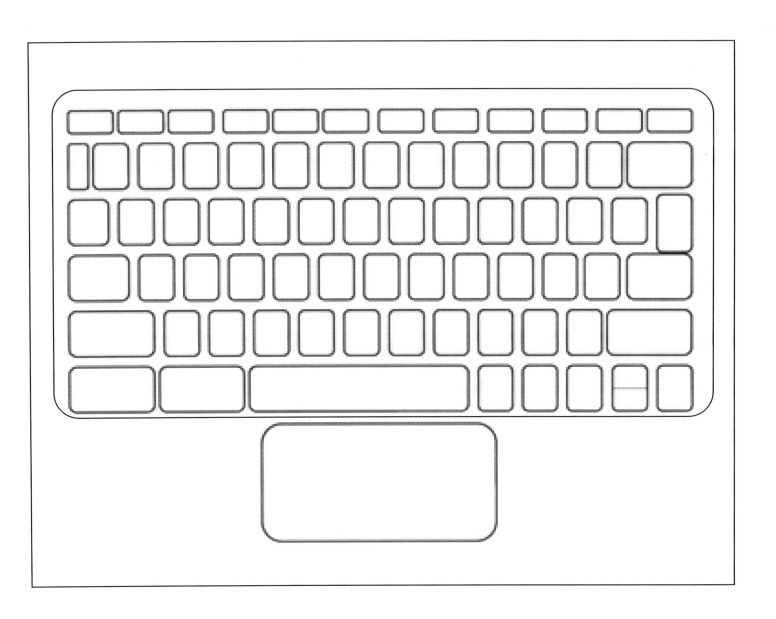

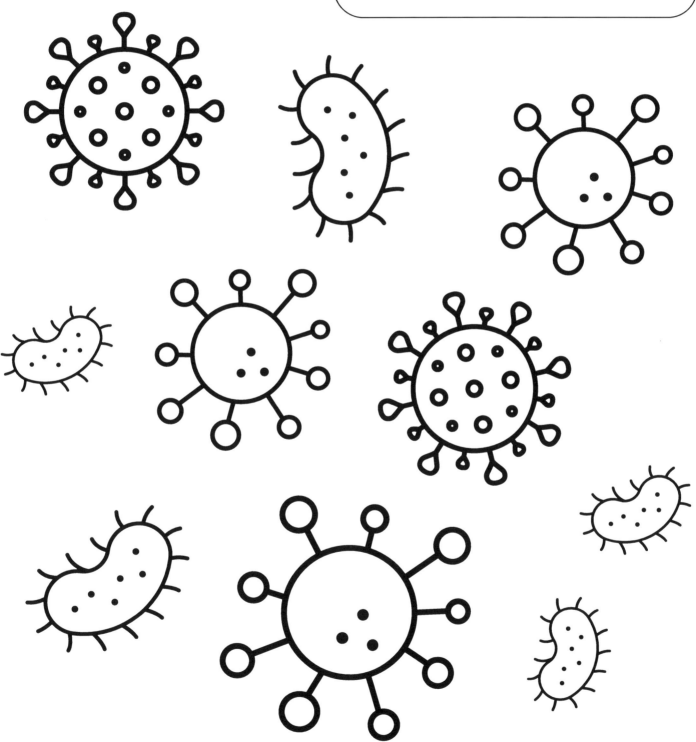

Eww Germs. Make them Beautiful Instead of Gross.

> Tell Me You Have Perfectionism without Telling Me You Have Perfectionism.

Make the Teeth Perfect!

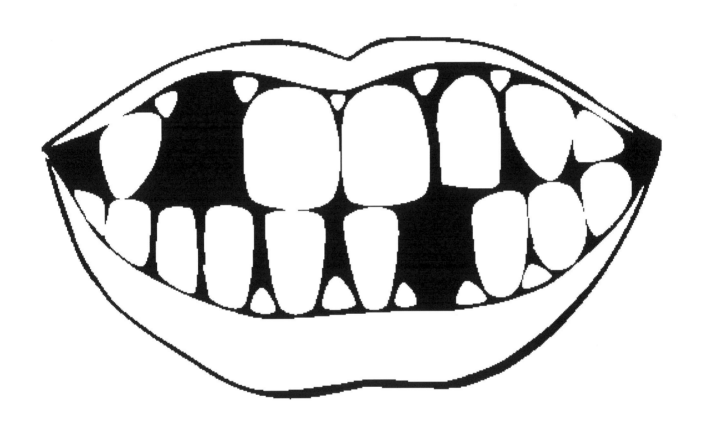

Grab Some Tape! Put 10 Pieces that are the Exact Same Size on This Page.

Fix the Eyebrows!

Put Four Circles Inside of the Circle Below. Make Sure they are Evenly Spaced.

Copy & Paste. Copy the Shape in The Box Below.

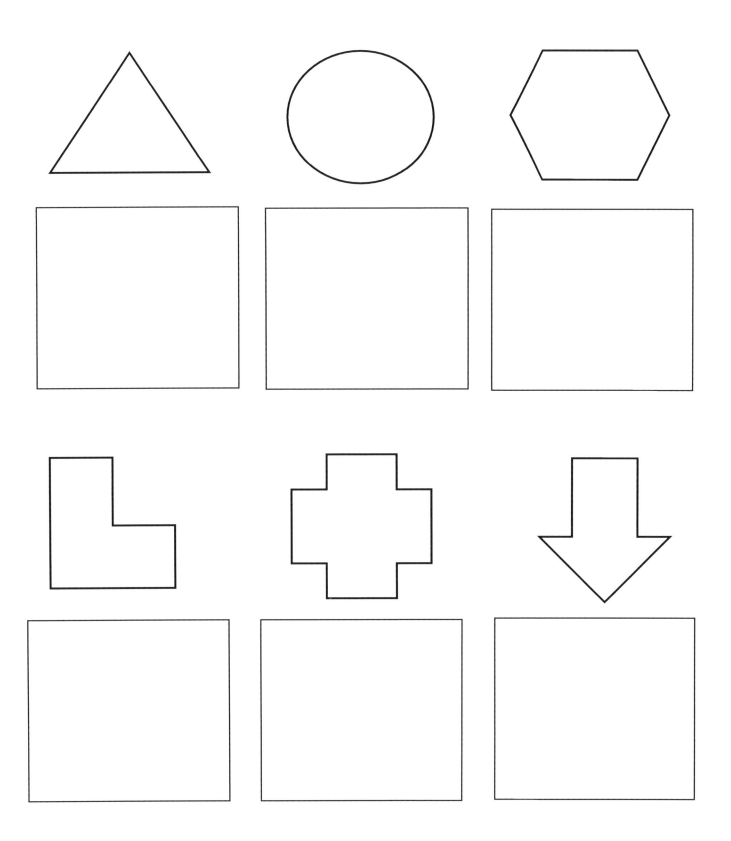

Color in This Entire Page with a Pencil. Use a Paper Towel to Smudge out the Imperfections.

Fill the Measuring Cup to Exactly Half.

Make This Entire Page Blue Using a Marker and ONLY Vertical Strokes.

What is Your Perfectionist Brain Always Telling You?

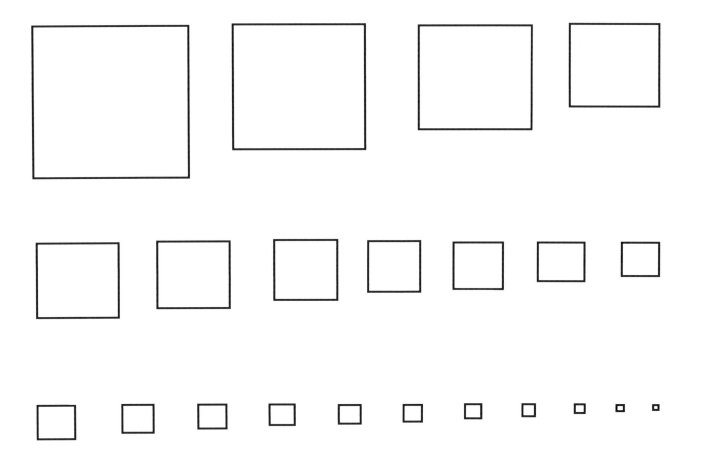

Color in All the Boxes! Start with the Biggest and End with the Smallest!

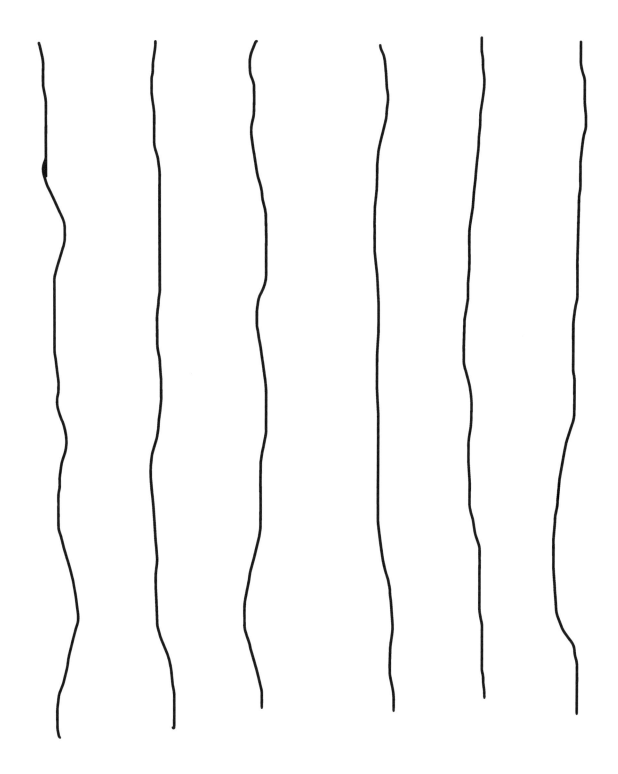

Make the Lines Perfect by Making Them Wider.

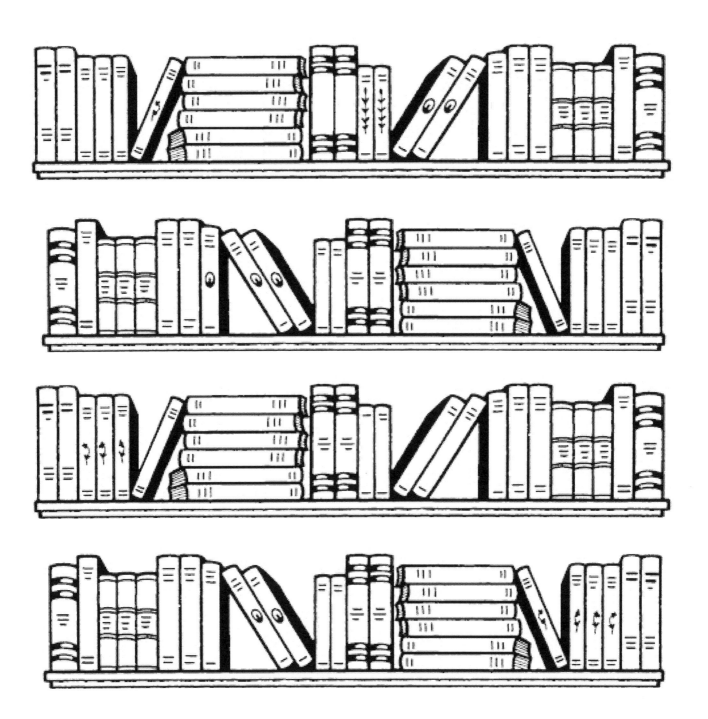

Color Coordinate This Book Library.

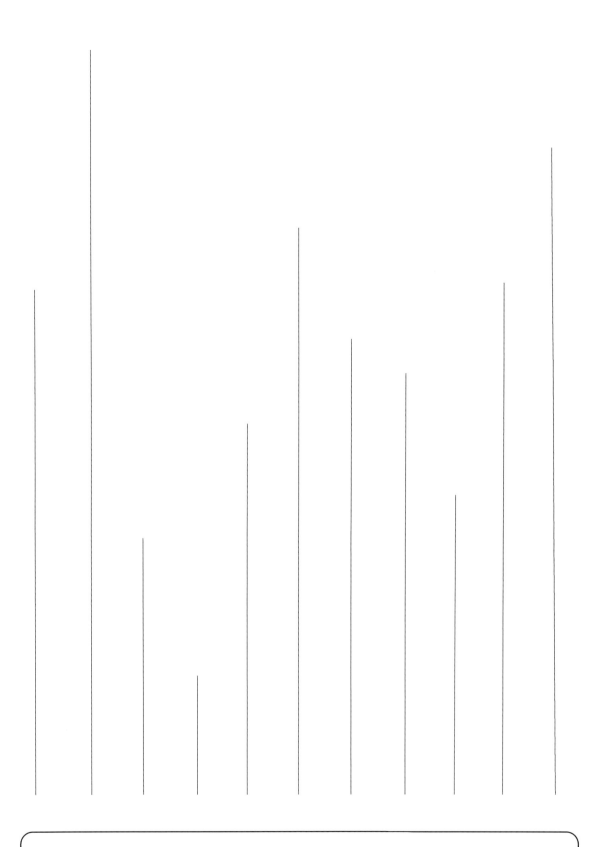

Make the Lines All the Same Height.

Turn This Box into Perfectly Spaced Stripes.

Make the Apples Whole Again.

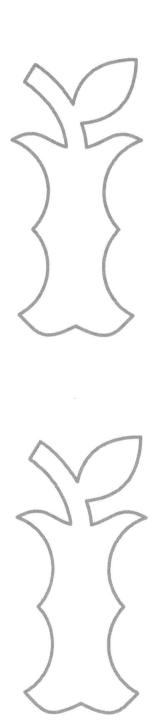

Start in the Middle and Draw a Line in Between the Spiral. Don't Touch the Edges!

Build Your Perfect Game Board!

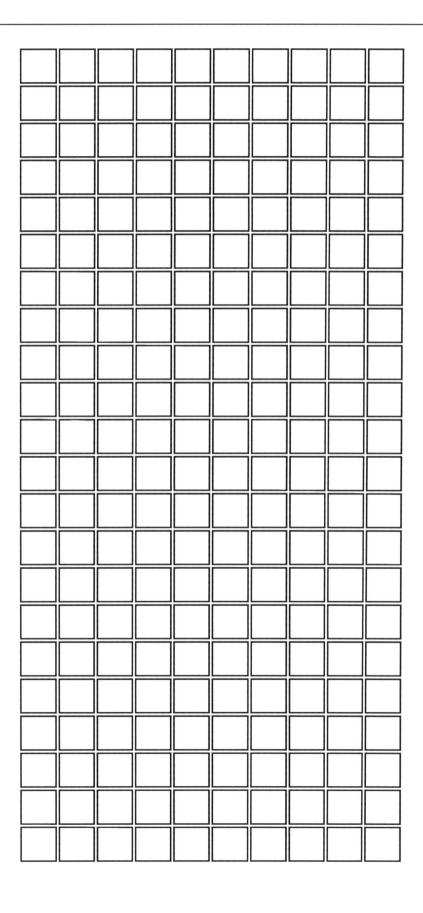

Fix The Arrows!

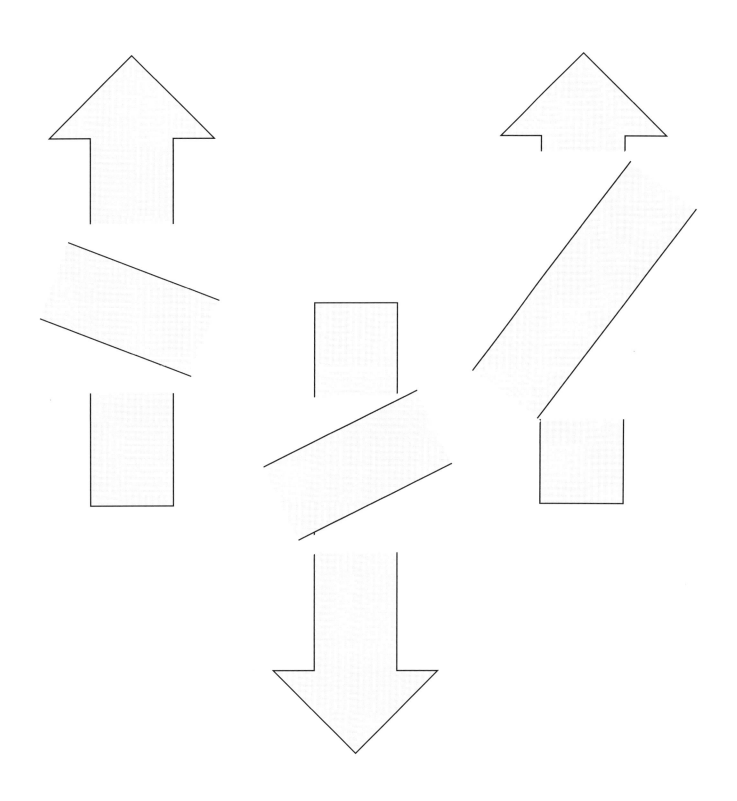

> Copy These Words Below in Their Exact Font.

Rainbow

Butterflies

MESSY

Clear His Complexion.

Clean up the Spill.

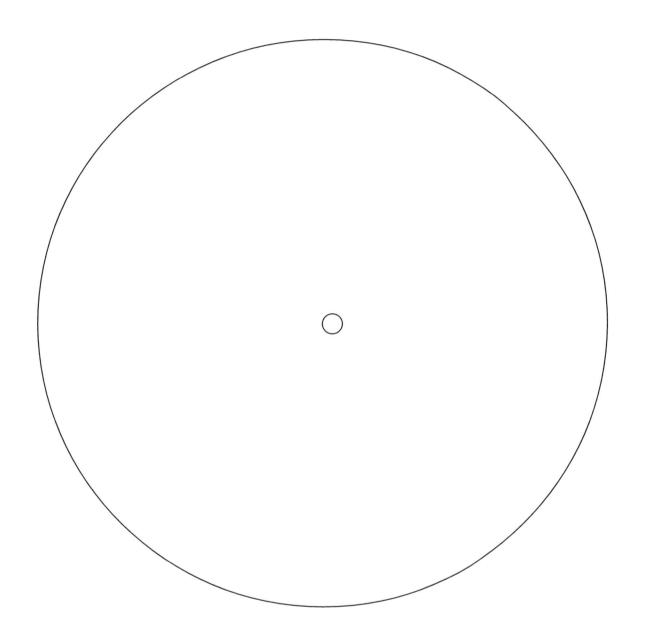

Create a Clock with Perfectly Spaced Numbers.

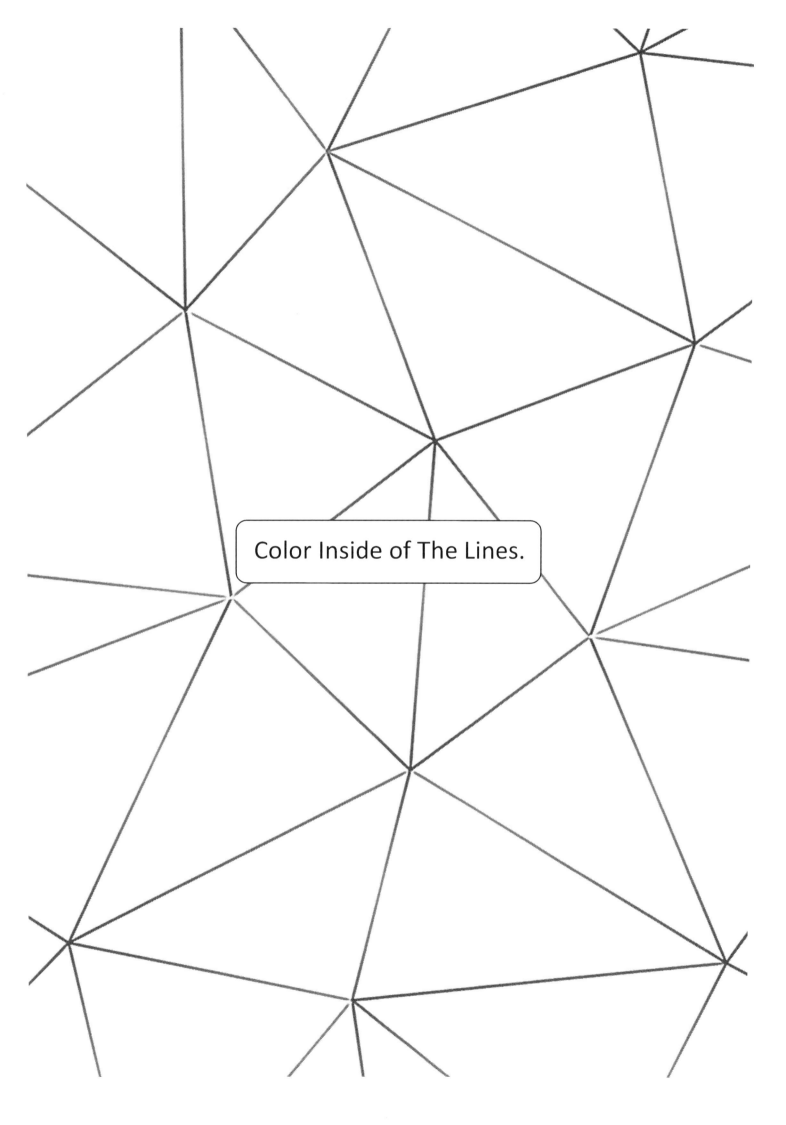

How Many ◯'s are on This Page?

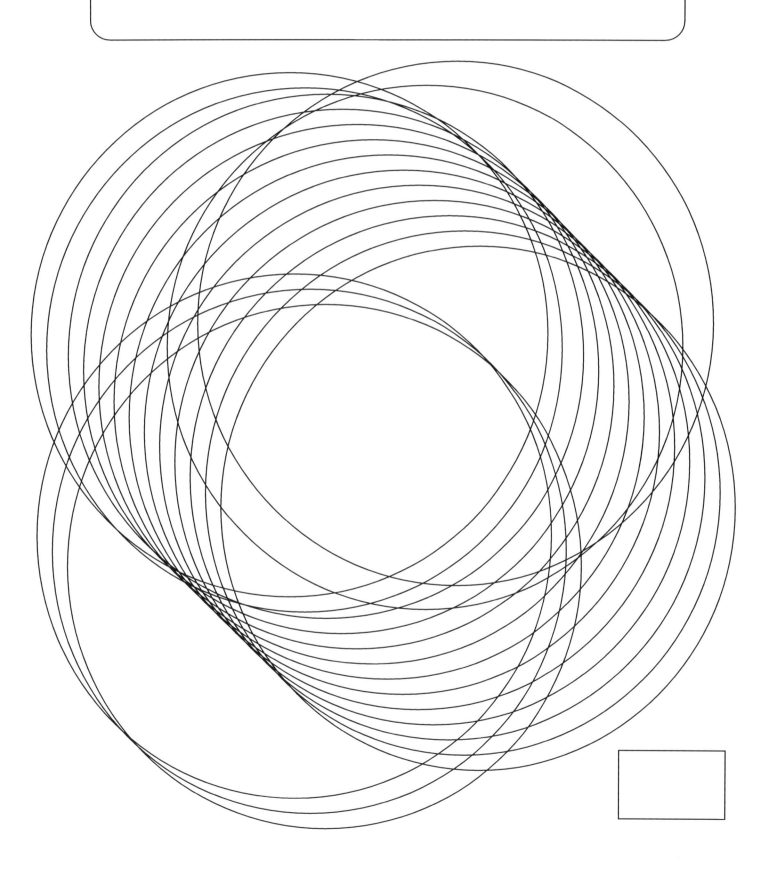

Create Something from These Accidental Scribbles.

 Every Snowflake Is Different but Make them All the Same.

Turn This into a Plaid Pattern.

Can You Find Them?

Sloth   Turtle   Monkey   Hamster   Goat

This Pizza Needs 8 Perfect Slices!

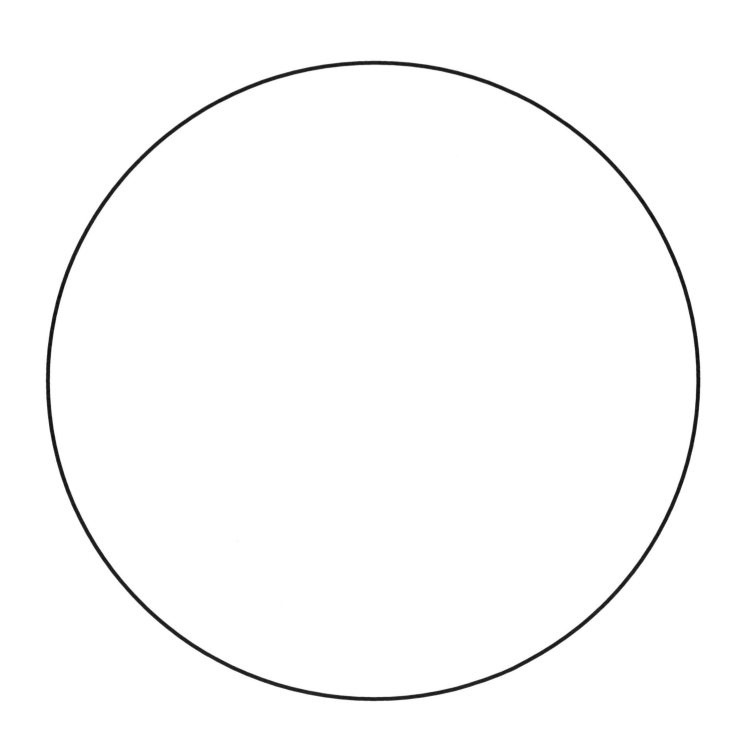

Check the Boxes! Make them All the Same.

Cut These Dotted Lines. Don't Go Outside of the Lines!

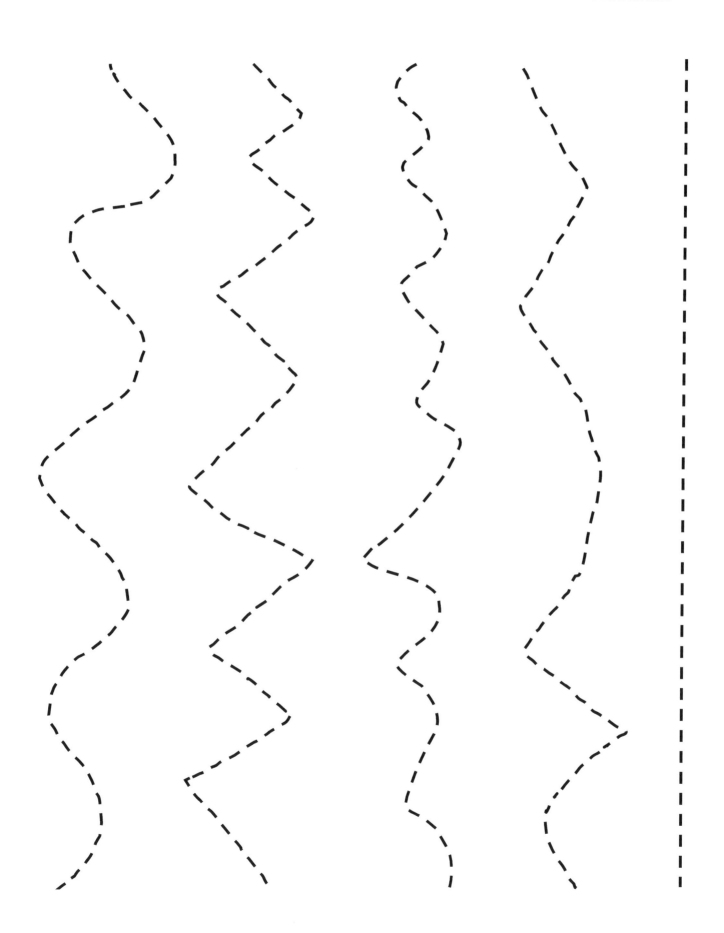

How Do You Like Your Lines in the Carpet?

Made in the USA
Monee, IL
20 February 2022